# LIBERTY LEGENDS ALPHABET

Words by Robin Feiner

**Aa**

**A** is for **A**braham Lincoln. As the 16th U.S. president, 'Honest Abe' kept the nation together during the American Civil War, and started the fight to end slavery in the United States. He is respected for his powerful persistence and belief in what was right.

Bb

B is for Ruth Bader Ginsburg. Before becoming a U.S. Supreme Court Justice, the 'Notorious RBG' spent her entire career fighting for gender equality and women's rights. Her early legal battles literally changed the world for women – legendary!

C is for Chief Joseph.
Standing true to his principles,
this masterful Native American
leader decided to retreat with
his Nez Perce tribe across the
Rocky Mountains in 1877.
He may have been forced to
surrender in the end, but he
fought honorably for
his people's freedom.

**D** is for **D**esmond Tutu. Renowned for defending the rights of the oppressed, this South African archbishop and humanitarian has been honored many times, with the Nobel Peace Prize in 1984, the U.S. Presidential Medal of Freedom in 2009, and the Gandhi Peace Prize in 2005, to name a few!

**Ee**

**E** is for **E**leanor Roosevelt. As the wife of U.S. President Franklin D. Roosevelt, this trailblazer was the first lady to redefine the role of First Lady! She embraced the media of the day, and gave a strong voice to the country's poor, oppressed and discriminated-against.

**F** is for Betty **F**riedan.
After no magazine would publish her article on women's aspirations outside the home, this groundbreaking feminist decided to write a book! 'The Feminine Mystique' became a landmark best-seller, and is said to have sparked the second wave of feminism in the U.S.

**Gg**

**G** is for Mohandas **G**andhi. Since leading his beloved India to independence in 1947, 'the great Mahatma' has been a symbol of peaceful strength all over the world. Renowned for his kindness and non-violent protests, his birthday (October 2) was declared International Day of Non-Violence.

**H is for Harvey Milk.** This California politician made history in 1977 when he became one of the first openly gay men elected to office. As a gay rights activist, he fought for equality for minorities, and was part of the legal LGBTQ-rights revolution that continues today.

I is for Ida B. Wells.
Born into slavery in 1862,
Ida became an early civil rights
leader. As a journalist, she
spoke out about racial injustice
as well as women's rights, and
was one of the founders of the
National Association for the
Advancement of Colored
People (NAACP). Legendary!

Jj

J is for John Lennon. Inviting people to 'Imagine' a place without war or injustice, this legendary Beatle protested for a peaceful world. Although some found his methods controversial, he stood up for what he believed in and dared to dream of better.

## Kk

**K** is for Dr. Martin Luther **K**ing Jr. He's the unmistakable face of the American civil rights movement. Fighting racism with the power of non-violent protest, his unforgettable 'I Have a Dream' speech inspired equality and justice for all. To honor his role in ending segregation, his birthday is a national U.S. holiday.

L is for the 14th Dalai Lama. Preaching inter-religious harmony and universal responsibility, His Holiness has spent his life serving the Tibetan people, and influencing all of humanity. He was awarded the Nobel Peace Prize in 1989 for his non-violent efforts to free Tibet, and his concern for global environmental issues.

**M** is for **M**alcolm X.
Battling prejudice and poverty
since his childhood, Malcolm
X became an influential
figure during the civil rights
movement in the U.S. An
outspoken, natural-born
leader, he fought for the
right of African Americans
to defend themselves against
discrimination.

Nn

N is for Nelson Mandela.
After spending 27 years
in prison for opposing South
Africa's racist government,
Mandela became the nation's
first black president. Fighting
inequality with forgiveness,
he led his country on its
long walk to freedom.
Truly inspirational!

Oo

**O** is for **O**skar Schindler. This German legend risked his own life to lead more than 1,200 Jews to safety during World War II. Thanks to his great courage and compassion, there are about 7,000 descendants of the Schindler Jews living in the U.S. and Europe today.

**P** is for Emmeline **P**ankhurst. Born in 1858, this trailblazer fought for and won women's right to vote during the British Suffragette movement. Urging women to demand their rights – rather than ask politely – Pankhurst shook society with her bold approach to change!

**Q is for Queen Nzinga of Angola. This 17th-century queen was one of the greatest female rulers of Africa, remembered for her courage and negotiation skills. Leading her troops in battle at the age of 60, she fought fearlessly for the freedom of her kingdoms.**

**R** is for **R**osa Parks.
When this 'first lady of civil rights' refused to give up her seat on a bus, she sparked the movement that eventually ended segregation in the United States. One single moment of courage that shaped a nation – legendary!

**S is for Sojourner Truth.** After escaping slavery in 1826, she traveled all over the U.S. to share her story and fight for the end of slavery. She also spoke out in support of women – her legendary speech 'Ain't I a Woman?' becoming a strong expression of women's rights.

Tt

**T** is for Harriet **T**ubman. Born into slavery, this courageous crusader escaped, then returned to lead other slaves to freedom. Nicknamed 'Moses,' she risked her own life to free more than 300 slaves in 10 years on the Underground Railroad – and "never lost a passenger." Legendary!

**U** is for **U2** frontman Bono. This Irish singer-songwriter is known as much for his lyrical genius as his social activism. Doing it all 'in the name of love,' he uses his music and fame to draw attention to important issues, such as the civil unrest in Ireland, and poverty and disease in Africa.

Vv

V is for Victoria Woodhull. This suffrage leader made history in 1872 when she became the first woman to run for president of the United States! She also fought for every woman's right to marry, divorce and have children without restriction. A legend ahead of her time!

**W** is for Sir **W**illiam Wallace. Considered Scotland's most patriotic hero, this brave knight put his country's liberty above everything. Going into battle for his nation's independence, sometimes outnumbered, Wallace is a legendary example of fighting fearlessly to protect the freedom of others.

Xx

**X is Liu Xiaobo.
Sometimes known as
'China's Nelson Mandela,'
Xiaobo fought for freedom
of speech in China for over
20 years. He was awarded
the Nobel Peace Prize in 2010
for "his long and non-violent
struggle for basic human
rights in China."**

Yy

**Y is for Malala Yousafzai.
Defending every girl's right
to an education made this
Pakistani schoolgirl a symbol
of courage and bravery
all over the world. As the
youngest person to ever
receive a Nobel Peace Prize,
Malala continues to be a voice
for young girls everywhere –
a living legend!**

**Z** is for Cesar Chave**z**. Even though many said it couldn't be done, Chavez set up a union in 1962 for American farmworkers battling low wages and harsh working conditions. He fought for the dignity of workers, and brought about great change for thousands of families.

# he ever-expanding
# gendary library

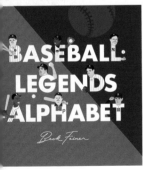

**XPLORE THESE LEGENDARY ALPHABETS & MORE AT WWW.ALPHABETLEGENDS.COM**

**LIBERTY LEGENDS ALPHABET**
www.alphabetlegends.com

Published by Alphabet Legends Pty Ltd in 2019
Created by Beck Feiner
Copyright © Alphabet Legends Pty Ltd 2019

**UNICEF AUSTRALIA**
A portion of the Net Proceeds from the sale of this book
are donated to UNICEF.

9780648506379